Kathy Schrock's
Every Day of the School Year Series

Teaching Language Arts Through Literature: Grades 4-6

by
Nancy J. Keane

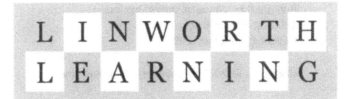

A Publication of Linworth Learning

Linworth Publishing, Inc.
Worthington, Ohio

To my children, Aureta and Alex Keane

And to the memory of my mother, Aureta C. Keane

Cataloging-in-Publication Data

Published by Linworth Publishing, Inc.
480 East Wilson Bridge Road, Suite L
Worthington, Ohio 43085

1-58683-106-2

5 4 3 2 1

Table of Contents

❖ Acknowledgments ❖

I wish to thank the people who have helped with this endeavor. First, I would like to thank all the authors who give us these marvelous stories to enjoy. With so many children's books in print, it was quite difficult to limit the entries in this book. Without these extraordinary people, this would have been an arduous task. As it was, I have spent numerous entertaining hours wrapped up in the books.

I would also like to thank the many librarians I have come in contact with. They have introduced me to books I might otherwise have missed. The library staff of the Concord (N.H.) School District has been very helpful, especially when I begged to borrow books from their collections. The staff of the Children's Room at Concord (N.H.) Public Library has also been helpful. Their fantastic collection kept me engrossed in quality literature for many, many days. They were particularly generous in retrieving books for me during their renovation when the books were not accessible to the public.

The many wonderful, dedicated teachers I have had the privilege of knowing also influenced this work tremendously. Their ideas for activities and their willingness to share helped a great deal. I have been very fortunate to work with a talented group of educators. Thanks especially to my editor, Kathy Schrock. She has been wonderfully supportive during this process.

Most importantly, I would like to thank my family. My children, Aureta and Alex, didn't complain too much about the amount of time I spent in the library or on the computer. They listened to the books I read to them and gave me their opinions on them. They understood when I would start booktalking a new book at seemingly random times. If you really want to know if a child will like a book, ask a child. My children are the best!

How to Use this Book

*A*nother school year begins. Another stretch of days to work with children is ahead. There is something very special about the beginning of the school year. We are looking forward to another year but also know we need to put together another year of lessons. Using children's literature in the classroom to introduce or extend classroom lessons is a proven way to get children involved. One way to excite children about reading is to use booktalks as hooks. Booktalks are short book promotions that tease the child into wanting to know more. Books that are not promoted often stay on the shelves to collect dust. When children hear about books either through friends or though booktalks, they are more apt to take them down and read them.

This book contains lesson ideas that are centered around themes and based on children's literature that is current or timeless. Children's literature has long been a vital part of every child's life. The stories often reflect society and help the child learn about his or her world. Children's literature shows children different perspectives from which they may experience events in a non-threatening way. Historical fiction introduces them to what life was like long ago, told in a way that is understandable to young children. By introducing children to different concepts via fiction, you can open the door to explore topics more in depth.

The purpose of this book is to promote fiction reading and to encourage the discussion to go further into real-life activities. The chapters are divided into topic areas. Each chapter includes a sample booktalk for that theme. A suggested booklist is included and sample activities follow.

The booktalks are in the form of short teasers to get the students interested in the books. These can be modified to reflect the needs of the population of children and the style of the booktalker. Information about the book includes author, title, publisher, date of publication, interest level (IL – given as grade level) and reading level (RL – given as grade level). The booktalk follows this bibliographic information.

The suggested book lists include books that reflect the theme of the chapter. The information given for each book includes author, title, publisher, date of publication, interest level (IL – given as grade level) and reading level (RL – given as grade level). In addition, a short annotation based on the Library of Congress summary statement is given.

Activities are included with each theme. These activities are samples and ideas of the type of things you may want to do with your students in order to follow up and expand upon the theme. They are just starters and leave plenty of room for you to personalize the activity.

The importance of reading has long been known to educators. In 1997, *President Clinton's Call to Action for American Education in the 21st Century* emphasized the importance of reading in the development of children. The document stressed the need for all fourth grade children to be able to read independently. Every state's educational standards also include an emphasis on independent reading as a standard to be addressed. The American Association of School Librarians, a division of the American Library Association, adopted their national standards, the *Information Power Standards,* in 1998. It is clear that the criteria for being an information literate person involve being able to read independently and being able to understand what is read. Children are often drawn more towards fiction for their reading choices. By using fiction as a springboard for learning, you will be able to help children connect reading for pleasure and reading for information.

Most states have adopted educational standards to ensure that all students are taught a common curriculum. Standards-based curriculum holds great potential for student achievement. For more than a decade, the Mid-continent Research for Education and Learning group (McREL) has been a recognized leader in developing K-12 standards for student achievement. Among their contributions to the education field is their compendium of K-12 standards. These standards can be accessed at http://www.mcrel.org. Throughout this book, the McREL standards are referenced within each chapter. Additionally, reference will be made when appropriate to the International Society for Technology in Education (ISTE) National Technology Education Standards (NETS). These standards can be viewed at http://cnets.iste.org

It is hoped classroom teachers, school librarians and media specialists, and public librarians will find inspiration in this book to use booktalking as a starting point for the discussion of themes. When children begin a lesson with enthusiasm, it's sure to be a hit!

To find out more about booktalking and to access a database of ready-to-use booktalks, visit the author's Web page ***Booktalks – Quick and Simple*** at http://www.nancykeane.com. The author has also set up a listserv to share and discuss booktalks. To join, simply visit ***Booktalks – Quick and Simple*** and click on "Join Booktalkers Group" or go to http://groups.yahoo.com/group/booktalkers/

About the Author

Nancy J. Keane is a school librarian in Concord, New Hampshire. She has been a lover of children's literature all her life, so working with books and children is a perfect match for her. In addition to her work in the school, Nancy also hosts a radio show on WKXL radio in Concord. *Kids Book Beat* is a monthly show that features children from the area booktalking about their favorite books. The show is live and unpredictable! Nancy also has authored a children's fiction book and several books on using booktalks.

Nancy is the author of an award-winning Web site, *Booktalks – Quick and Simple*, at <http://www.nancykeane.com/booktalks/>. The site logs about 500 hits a day and has proven to be indispensable to librarians and teachers. The database includes more than 1,000 ready-to-use booktalks and welcomes contributions from educators. Additionally, Nancy has set up a listserv to bring together people who want to discuss booktalking and share booktalks. This list welcomes new members and may be joined by contacting booktalkers@yahoogroups.com.

Nancy received a B.A. from the University of Massachusetts, Amherst, an M.L.S. from the University of Rhode Island, and an M.A. in Educational Technology from George Washington University. She is an adjunct faculty member at New Hampshire Technical College, Connected University, and she teaches workshops for the University of New Hampshire.

Nancy lives in Concord, New Hampshire, with her children, Aureta and Alex. They share their home with their dog and four cats.

A Word From
❖ Kathy Schrock ❖

elcome to the Every Day of the School Year Series. As an educator, library media specialist, and now technology administrator, I know how important it is for the classroom teacher to extend the learning experiences in the classroom. With the current focus on standards-based teaching, learning, and assessment, I felt it was important to supply classroom teachers and library media specialists with activities that directly support the curriculum, but at the same time allow for creative teachers to supplement and extend activities for their students.

The activities in this series are varied in scope, but all of them provide practical tips, tricks, ideas, activities and units. Many of the activities include related print and Internet sites that are easily collected by the classroom teacher before engaging in the activity. There are handouts, worksheets, and much more throughout the books, too.

In my job as technology administrator for a school district, I am often able to plan lessons with teachers and visit classrooms to observe the teaching of the lesson. In addition, as the creator and maintainer, since 1995, of Kathy Schrock's Guide for Educators (http://discoveryschool.com/schrockguide/), a portal of categorized Web sites for teachers, I often receive e-mail from teachers who are searching for practical, creative, and easy-to-implement activities for the classroom. I hope this series provides just the impetus for you to stretch and enhance your textbook, lesson, and standards-based unit by use of these activities.

If you have any titles you would like to see added to the series, or would like to author yourself, drop me a note at kathy@kathyschrock.net

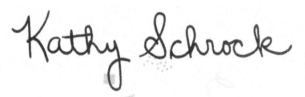

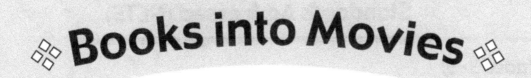

Books into Movies

Introduction

Lights, camera, action! Making a movie is exciting and a lot of work. Some of our favorite books are made into movies for us to enjoy. Sometimes we are happy with the results, but sometimes we like the book much better. Sometimes the movie seems to have nothing to do with the book other than the title. Let's look at some well-known children's literature that has graced the silver screen. Some of these you have probably seen in the movie theater. Others you may have seen on video. And still others may be on your list to see someday. In the meantime, let's talk about making books into movies.

Standards Addressed (McREL)
Language Arts
Media
Standard 10

Understands the characteristics and components of the media

Level II Grade: 3-5

4. Understands that media messages and products are composed of a series of separate elements (e.g., shots in movies, sections of a newspaper)

Viewing
Standard 9

Uses viewing skills and strategies to understand and interpret visual media

Level II Grade: 3-5

1. Understands different messages conveyed through visual media (e.g., main ideas and supporting details; facts and opinions; main characters, setting, and sequence of events in visual narratives)

2. Understands techniques used to convey messages in visual media (e.g., animation; different tones of voice in audio productions; adjusting messages for different audiences)

3. Knows that film and television have features that identify different genres (e.g., style of dress, setting in a western or a drama)

5. Understands techniques used to establish mood in visual media (e.g., use of camera angles and distances to create a specific feeling or point of view, tension heightened by dramatic music, sound effects such as a heartbeat or squeaking chair, use of a deep voice, somber lighting to imply mystery or fear)

Standards Addressed (NETS)
Performance Indicators for Technology-Literate Students

Grades 3–5:

4. Use general purpose productivity tools and peripherals to support personal productivity, remediate skill deficits, and facilitate learning throughout the curriculum

5. Use technology tools (e.g., multimedia authoring, presentation, Web tools, digital cameras, scanners) for individual and collaborative writing, communication, and publishing activities to create knowledge products for audiences inside and outside the classroom

6. Use telecommunications efficiently to access remote information, communicate with others in support of direct and independent learning, and pursue personal interests

Sample Booktalk:

Norton, Mary. *The Borrowers*. New York: Harcourt Brace, 1953. IL 5-8, RL 5.9

Have you ever lost something in your house? Maybe a sock or a notebook? You know just where you put it but it just isn't there. Keys are a commonly misplaced item. But are they really misplaced or did someone borrow them? Perhaps there is someone in your home who likes to borrow things from people. Is there a "borrower" in your home? A borrower is a tiny person who lives hidden in your home. The borrowers might live behind the walls, in the cabinets or even under the floor. They live by borrowing from the humans in the house. That's how they get their food, clothes and even their furniture. The very worst possible thing that can happen to a borrower is to be seen by a human. They take great care not to be seen while out on a borrowing expedition. But in this case, Homily and Pad Clock discover that their daughter has not only been seen by a human, she has spoken with one! The human family decides they must rid their home of the little people. This forces the little family to leave their comfortable home under the clock and seek out a new home. Can the human child protect them? Can they learn to live in peace even after being seen? And have you lost anything in your home lately? Perhaps you have a clan of borowers living hidden in your home.

Book List:

Dahl, Roald. *Charlie and the Chocolate Factory.* New York: Knopf, Distributed by Random House, 1973, c1964, IL 3-6, RL 5.9
Each of five children lucky enough to discover an entry ticket into Mr. Willy Wonka's mysterious chocolate factory takes advantage of the situation in his own way.

Dahl, Roald. *Matilda*. New York: Viking, c1988, IL 3-6, RL 5.2
Matilda applies her untapped mental powers to rid the school of the evil, child-hating headmistress, Miss Trunchbull, and restore her nice teacher, Miss Honey, to financial security.

Dalgliesh, Alice, *The Courage of Sarah Noble*. New York: Atheneum Books for Young Readers, c1986, c1954, IL 3-6, RL 4.4
Remembering her mother's words, an eight-year-old girl finds courage to go alone with her father to build a new home in the Connecticut wilderness and to stay with the Indians when her father goes back to bring the rest of the family.

Fitzhugh, Louise. *Harriet, the Spy*. New York: Dell Yearling, 2001, c1964, IL 5-8, RL 5.9
Eleven-year-old Harriet keeps notes on her classmates and neighbors in a secret notebook, but when some of the students read the notebook, they seek revenge.

Juster, Norton. *The Phantom Tollbooth.* New York: Random House, c1961, IL 5-8, RL 5.4
A journey through a land where Milo learns the importance of words and numbers provides a cure for his boredom.

King-Smith, Dick. *Babe: The Gallant Pig.* New York: Crown, 1985, c1983, IL 3-6, RL 5.8
A piglet destined for butchering arrives at the farmyard, is adopted by an old sheep dog, and discovers a special secret to success.

MacLachlan, Patricia. *Sarah, Plain and Tall.* New York: Charlotte Zolotow Book, c1985, IL 3-6, RL 4.2
When their father invites a mail-order bride to come live with them in their prairie home, Caleb and Anna are captivated by their new mother and hope that she will stay.

Montgomery, L. M. *Anne of Green Gables.* New York: Knopf, Distributed by Random House, 1995, IL 5-8, RL 7.2
Anne, an 11-year-old orphan, is sent by mistake to live with a lonely middle-aged brother and sister on a Prince Edward Island farm and proceeds to make an indelible impression on everyone around her.

Philbrick, W. R. *Freak the Mighty.* New York: Scholastic, c1993, IL 5-8, RL 6.3
At the beginning of eighth grade, learning-disabled Max and his new friend, Freak, whose birth defect has affected his body but not his brilliant mind, find when they combine forces they make a powerful team.

White, E. B. *Stuart Little.* New York: HarperCollins, c1973, IL 3-6, RL 5.4
This book chronicles the adventures of the mouse, Stuart Little, as he sets out in the world to find his dearest friend, a little bird who stayed a few days in his family's garden.

Suggested Activities:

Activity #1: **Same or Different**

Have students brainstorm books the class has read that have been turned into movies. Which ones have the students seen? Do the movies follow the same plot as the book? If not, where do you think they differ? Can you think why the moviemakers would change the plot? You may want to use a three-column chart to record their thoughts.

Activity #2: **You Ought To Be in Pictures**

Brainstorm books the class has read that have not been turned into movies. Which books do you think would make good movies? What is there about the book that you think will make it a good movie?

Activity #3: **Seen Any Good Pictures Lately?**

When the students have finished reading a book and watching the movie based on the book, have them write a letter to a friend telling which they prefer. Questions they might want to answer: Why do you like one better than the other? What are good points about each? What didn't you like about each? Would you recommend that your friend read the book before seeing the movie? Why or why not?

Activity #4: **Casting Call**

Tell the students they have been chosen to cast a new movie based on a book they have read. Their job is to cast the actors to play the main characters from the book. Who would you chose and why? See Handout #1: *Cast of Characters.*

Handout #1: Cast of Characters

Title of Book: _____

Character Name	Actor	Reasons

Activity #5: **Hollywood Scriptwriter**

You have been asked by a major motion picture company to help them bring one of your favorite books to the screen. They are hiring you and your group members to write a script for one scene of the book. Choose and read the scene from the book carefully. Where does it take place? Inside or outside? Time of year? What characters are in the scene? What is the major theme of the scene? What is the mood? Be sure to notice the actions of the characters as well so they can be written into the scene.

Working in groups, students will create a script for one scene of a book. If all students are using the same book, they can be given different scenes so that a script can be written for a larger part of the book. Be sure the students write the dialog as well as stage directions. This is easily done in a two-column format with character dialog on the left and stage directions on the right. They should give an overview of what the scenery is like and who is in the scene. The students can even take different roles for the project such as screenwriter, director, and stage hand. See Handout #2: *Script Handout*.

Handout #2: Script Handout

Title of Book: _____

Dialog	Stage Directions

Bullies

Introduction

Unfortunately everyone will encounter a bully sometime in his or her life. Some of us find ourselves being picked on more than others. Children need to learn why bullying is wrong. They also need to learn strategies for coping with bullying behavior and how to avoid it in themselves. Using children's literature can help students define and learn to deal with bullying behavior. All of these fiction books feature bullies and demonstrate differing approaches to handling the situation.

Standards Addressed (McREL)
Reading
Standard 6
Uses reading skills and strategies to understand and interpret a variety of literary texts

Level II Grade: 3-5

5. Understands elements of character development in literary works (e.g., differences between main and minor characters; stereotypical characters as opposed to fully developed characters; changes that characters undergo; the importance of a character's actions, motives, and appearance to plot and theme)

6. Makes inferences or draws conclusions about characters' qualities and actions (e.g., based on knowledge of plot, setting, characters' motives, characters' appearances, other characters' responses to a character)

9. Makes connections between characters or simple events in a literary work and people or events in his or her own life

Health
Standard 5
Knows essential concepts and practices concerning injury prevention and safety

Level II Grade: 3-5

4. Knows the difference between positive and negative behaviors used in conflict situations

5. Knows some nonviolent strategies to resolve conflicts

Standards Addressed (NETS)
Performance Indicators for Technology-Literate Students

Grades 3-5

4. Use general purpose productivity tools and peripherals to support personal productivity, remediate skill deficits, and facilitate learning throughout the curriculum

5. Use technology tools (e.g., multimedia authoring, presentation, Web tools, digital cameras, scanners) for individual and collaborative writing, communication, and publishing activities to create knowledge products for audiences inside and outside the classroom.

6. Use telecommunications efficiently to access remote information, communicate with others in support of direct and independent learning, and pursue personal interests.

Sample Booktalk:

Myers, Laurie; illustrated by Dan Yaccarino. *Surviving Brick Johnson.* New York: Clarion Books, 2000. IL 3-6, RL 3.5

At the dinner table, Mom asked each of us to tell about one good thing and one bad thing that happened at school that day. Liz is really caught up in the middle school thing so both her good thing and her bad thing were the same: Andrew Marshall asked her out. Girls! Bob told about being spit on by a girl. Oh, to be in first grade again where the worst thing that could happen to you was to be spit on. When it got to my turn, my bad thing was that Brick Johnson was going to maim me! Well, he didn't actually say it but everyone knows that's what he meant. So tonight I start karate lessons. That's the only way I can be safe. The first thing the karate teacher tells me is to make your enemy your friend. No thanks! My life depends on Surviving Brick Johnson.

Book List:

Dadey, Debbie. *King of the Kooties.* New York: Walker & Co, 1999. IL 3-6, RL 4.0
Nate's new friend, Donald, is being teased by the meanest girl in fourth grade, but after several failed attempts, he comes up with a plan to make her stop.

Duncan, Lois. *Wonder Kid Meets the Evil Lunch Snatcher.* Boston: Little, Brown, c1988. IL 3-6, RL 4.7
Terrorized by an evil lunch-snatcher at his new school, Brian devises, with the help of a fellow comic book fan, a plan involving a new super hero called Wonder Kid.

Hahn, Mary Downing. *Stepping on the Cracks.* New York: Clarion, 1991. IL 3-6, RL 6.3
In 1944, while her brother is overseas fighting in World War II, 11-year-old Margaret gets a new view of the school bully, Gordy, when she finds him hiding his own brother, an army deserter, and decides to help him.

Krensky, Stephen. *Louise Takes Charge.* New York: Dial Books for Young Readers, c1998. IL 3-6, RL 5.2
Louise enlists the aid of everyone in her class and together they outwit Jasper the bully.

McNamee, Graham. *Nothing Wrong with a Three-Legged Dog.* New York: Delacorte Press, 2000. IL 3-5, RL 4.5
With the help of his good friend and her three-legged dog, Leftovers, 10-year-old Keath learns how to handle the class bully and deal with being the only white boy in his class.

Mead, Alice. *Junebug and the Reverend.* New York: Farrar Straus Giroux, 1998. IL 3-6, RL 4.2
Having moved out of the housing project and into a new home along with his mother and sister, 10-year-old Junebug discovers that bullies are everywhere and the elderly can make great friends.

Moss, Marissa. *Amelia Takes Command.* Middleton, WI: Pleasant Co. Publications, 1999. IL 3-6, RL 4.2
After successfully commanding the Discovery shuttle mission at Space Camp, Amelia returns to fifth grade where she deals with the bully who has been making her life miserable.

Roberts, Willo Davis. *The Kidnappers: A Mystery*. New York: Atheneum Books for Young Readers, c1998. (IL 3-6, RL 5.9)
No one believes 11-year-old Joey, who has a reputation for telling tall tales, when he claims to have witnessed the kidnapping of the class bully outside their expensive New York City private school.

Shreve, Susan Richards. *Joshua T. Bates Takes Charge*. New York: Knopf, 1997, c1993. IL 3-6, RL 5.6
Eleven-year-old Joshua, worried about fitting in at school, feels awkward when the new student he is supposed to be helping becomes the target of the fifth grade's biggest bully.

Sonenklar, Carol. *Mighty Boy*. New York: Orchard, c1999. IL 3-6, RL 5.0
When he gets a chance to meet his hero, the television character Mighty Boy, Howard Weinstein discovers his own strengths that help him handle the bully in his new fourth grade class.

Suggested Activities:

Activity #1: What Is a Bully?

Have students brainstorm the characteristics of a bully. Have them search for common traits all bullies share. Have the class come up with a definitive list of bullying traits and write about a time they may have exhibited one of these traits.

Activity #2: A Bully from All Angles

Rewrite the bullying story from another character's perspective. Have one group of students retell the story from the bully's point of view as another group retells the story from the victim's point of view. The third group should retell it from a bystander's point of view. What do these different perspectives tell us?

Activity #3: Readers' Theater

Choose a scene from the book and rewrite it as reader's theater. Have students act out the story. After others are given the opportunity to comment on the different behaviors, make a chart of appropriate behaviors and inappropriate behaviors. Brainstorm ideas for dealing with a bully. What can the children do when they run into a bully?

Resources available on Readers' Theater:

http://www.aaronshep.com/rt/

http://www.loiswalker.com/catalog/teach.html

http://www.geocities.com/Athens/Thebes/9893/readerstheater.htm

Activity #4: Puzzle Me This

Using the characteristics of a bully that were decided on by the class, have students create cross-word puzzles or word search puzzles. Students can use the Puzzlemaker Web site found at http://puzzlemaker.discoveryschool.com

Activity #5: Banishing the Bully Board Game

1. Before students begin writing questions for this trivia game, encourage them to use two different types of questions (*inference questions and recall questions*) in order to make the game more challenging. Explain to students **recall questions** are factual questions that have only one answer (e.g. What is the most common behavior of a bully? Should you hold the door open for a classmate?) **Inference questions**, however, are questions that require an opinion as an answer (e.g. Why do bullies behave as they do?) Since this type of question can have more than one correct answer, explain to students a correct answer to an inference question is one in which the answer is supported by facts from the book.

2. Break students into small groups and ask them to create a stack of inference and recall question cards on index cards. Have them put the question on one side of the index card and the answer on the other.

3. Once those have been completed, have each group create a game board and write up a set of simple rules for their bullying games.

4. Once they have created the games, allow the groups to switch and play each other's games.

Community Involvment

Introduction

As children grow within their community, they begin to understand what it means to be part of a community; they recognize their place within it. They understand they need to contribute to their community as well as take from it. They learn to respect the rules and the people involved in the community. In this chapter, we look at books that feature characters contributing to their community in both small and large ways. The activities revolve around ways to contribute to the local community.

Standards Addressed
Language Arts
Reading
Standard 6

Uses reading skills and strategies to understand and interpret a variety of literary texts

Level II Grade: 3–5

5. Understands elements of character development in literary works (e.g., differences between main and minor characters; stereotypical characters as opposed to fully developed characters; changes that characters undergo; the importance of a character's actions, motives, and appearance to plot and theme)

7. Knows themes that recur across literary works

Thinking and Reasoning
Standard 5

Applies basic trouble-shooting and problem-solving techniques

Level II Grade: 3–5

1. Identifies issues and problems in the school or community that one might help solve

2. Studies problems in the community and how they were solved

Standard 6

Applies decision-making techniques

Level II Grade: 3–5

1. Studies decisions that were made in the community in terms of the alternatives that were considered

Standards Addressed (NETS)
Performance Indicators for Technology-Literate Students

Grades 3-5

4. Use general purpose productivity tools and peripherals to support personal productivity, remediate skill deficits, and facilitate learning throughout the curriculum

5 Use technology tools (e.g., multimedia authoring, presentation, Web tools, digital cameras, scanners) for individual and collaborative writing, communication, and publishing activities to create knowledge products for audiences inside and outside the classroom

6. Use telecommunications efficiently to access remote information, communicate with others in support of direct and independent learning, and pursue personal interests

Sample Booktalk:

Fleischman, Paul. *Seedfolks*. New York: HarperCollins, c1997, IL 5-8, RL 5.0

Have you ever thought about doing something in your community but thought you couldn't make much of an impact? After all, what can one person do? Well, maybe one person can make a start! Kim is living in a trash-filled inner-city neighborhood. When her father dies, she is determined to find a way to keep his memory alive. She plants some lima beans in the vacant lot. Others in the neighborhood see this and begin to follow her example. As others plant their own seeds for their own purposes, the vacant lot is transformed into a lovely garden. But what of the people who do the planting? How are their lives changed by this experience? Harvest a great story by reading Seedfolks by Paul Fleischman.

Book List:

Bonners, Susan. *Edwina Victorious*. New York: Farrar Straus Giroux, 2000, IL 3-6, RL 4.6
Edwina follows in the footsteps of her namesake great-aunt when she begins to write letters to the mayor about community problems and poses as Edwina the elder.

DiCamillo, Kate. *Because of Winn-Dixie*. Cambridge, Mass.: Candlewick Press, 2000, IL 3-6, RL 5.8
Ten-year-old India Opal Buloni describes her first summer in the town of Naomi, Florida, and all the good things that happen to her because of her big ugly dog, Winn-Dixie.

Greenwald, Sheila. *My Fabulous New Life*. San Diego: Browndeer Press , Harcourt Brace & Co, c1993, IL 3-6, RL 4.4
Eleven-year-old Alison has moved from the affluent suburbs to an apartment in New York City, where she tries to make new friends and come to terms with the homelessness she sees all around her.

Hamilton, Morse. *The Garden of Eden Motel*. New York: Greenwillow Books, c1999, IL 5-8, RL 6.0
In the early 1950s, 11-year-old Dal accompanies his stepfather, Mr. Sabatini, on a business trip to a rural community in Idaho, where Dal makes new friends and becomes involved in a scheme involving a uranium mine.

Haugaard, Kay. *No Place*. Minneapolis, MN: Emeryville, Calif.: Milkweed Editions, Distributed by Publishers Group West, 1998, IL 3-6, RL 5.9
Twelve-year-old Arturo has no place to play in his run-down inner-city Los Angeles neighborhood, so Arturo and the other students in his sixth-grade class raise money and build a park. In the process, they learn lessons about hard work, creativity, and teamwork.

Klass, Sheila Solomon. *Little Women Next Door*. New York: Holiday House, c2000, IL 3-6, RL 4.6
This novel recounts the efforts of Louisa May Alcott's family to establish a utopian community known as Fruitlands in Massachusetts in 1843, as seen through the eyes of the shy 11-year-old girl next door.

Koertge, Ronald. *The Heart Of The City*. New York: Orchard Books, c1998, IL 3-6, RL 4.8
After she and her parents move to an ethnically-mixed inner city neighborhood, 10-year-old Joy and her new friend Neesha decide to do something to keep drug dealers off their block.

Pellegrino, Marjorie White. *My Grandma's the Mayor*. Washington, DC: Magination Press, c2000, IL 3-6, RL 4.8
Annie is unhappy that she has to share her grandmother, the mayor, with so many people, but when she helps out during a town emergency, Annie appreciates all that her grandmother does in the community.

Whitworth, Artie. *Turkey John*. Prairie Grove, AR: Ozark Pub, c1995, IL 3-6, RL 6.2
Turkey John and the other people living in a rural community in southwestern Oklahoma during the Great Depression manage to survive by working hard and helping one another.

Williams, Laura E. *Up a Creek*. New York: H. Holt, 2001, IL 5-8, RL 5.8
Thirteen-year-old Starshine Bott learns how to cope with an unconventional, politically active mother and does a lot of growing up in the process.

Suggested Activities:

Activity #1: My Neighborhood

Students will learn more about their own community by identifying specific characteristics of their own neighborhood. They will share these observations with the class. This activity helps students understand there are many neighborhoods that make up their community and that these neighborhoods may have similarities as well as differences. Find out which community organizations may offer services to different areas of the community.

Activity #2: Community Brochure

What makes your community a good place to live? Brainstorm ideas with the students. Then have students create a brochure that will encourage people to visit their community. Have them highlight cultural activities, recreational activities, and anything that makes their community unique.

Activity #3: Adopt-a-Spot

Every community has an area in need of some extra care. This spot could be a park or an area around the school. Have the children "adopt-a-spot" to care for. This can be a one-time activity or an ongoing project.

The Adopt-A-Spot program enables organizations to maintain various city squares, monuments and historical markers, guardrails and landscaped traffic islands. Volunteers perform routine maintenance such as mowing, weeding, litter removal, landscape plantings, painting, and in some cases, minor repairs. Consult with city officials to be sure the area is safe and an appropriate place for children to work.

Activity #4: Community Service Map

■ Students will research community service organizations in their area.

■ Students will list the organizations noting

- ▶ Name of organization
- ▶ Mission
- ▶ Address
- ▶ Telephone number

- Students will categorize the organizations into a logical system (e.g. medical, housing, mental health).

- Students will color code the organizations based on category.

- Students will place color icons on the community map.

- Students will create a legend explaining the icons and listing the organizations.

- As a community service, students may even create a Web page with this information.

Activity #5: Postage Stamp

Many people contribute to the well-being of a community. Some may give a bit more than others. Have the students think of a person within their community who contributes to make it a better place. They will then design a postage stamp to honor that special person. They will need to explain why that person makes a difference in their community. See Handout #3: *Postage Stamps*.

Handout #3: Postage Stamps

Dragons, Unicorns and Mythical Beasts

Introduction

Fire breathing dragons. Beautiful unicorns. Animals with magical powers. These are all creatures that send our imaginations into overdrive. Children love reading about animals with magical powers. In this chapter, we fly away with some unicorns, dragons, a kraken and even a mermaid or two. Let their imaginations run wild, as wild as these animals. Then spend some time with the classroom activities.

Standards Addressed (McREL)
Languge Arts
Reading
Standard 6
Uses reading skills and strategies to understand and interpret a variety of literary texts

Level II Grade: 3-5

1. Uses reading skills and strategies to understand a variety of literary passages and texts (e.g., fairy tales, folk tales, fiction, nonfiction, myths, poems, fables, fantasies, historical fiction, biographies, autobiographies, chapter books)

2. Knows the defining characteristics of a variety of literary forms and genres (e.g., fairy tales, folk tales, fiction, nonfiction, myths, poems, fables, fantasies, historical fiction, biographies, autobiographies, chapter books)

Standards Addressed (NETS)
Performance Indicators for Technology-Literate Students

Grades 3-5

4. Use general purpose productivity tools and peripherals to support personal productivity, remediate skill deficits, and facilitate learning throughout the curriculum

5. Use technology tools (e.g., multimedia authoring, presentation, Web tools, digital cameras, scanners) for individual and collaborative writing, communication, and publishing activities to create knowledge products for audiences inside and outside the classroom

6. Use telecommunications efficiently to access remote information, communicate with others in support of direct and independent learning, and pursue personal interests

Sample Booktalk:

Ibbotson Eva. *Island Of The Aunts*. New York: Dutton Children's Books, 2000. IL 3-6, RL 4.8

Minette, Fabio and Lambert have some very unusual aunts. Maybe some of you have relatives who you think are a bit odd, too. Do you? Well, I bet none of your relatives are like aunts Etta, Coral and

Myrtle. These three are caretakers on a very special island. They care for the animals and tend to all the chores themselves. They are getting older, though, and are starting to have a hard time keeping all the animals safe. They can't just go out and hire some help here on this island. They need to keep their animals away from most people. After all, what would people say if they saw a mermaid? Or a little kraken? Or boobrie that lays eggs so big that just one egg makes 72 omelets? You can tell there are very special inhabitants on the island. So what can the aunts do to get some help? They decide to kidnap some help, of course! That's been the way it's always been done. They set out to kidnap Minette, Fabio and Lambert. What will happen? Will the children go to the island? Will the animals be taken care of? To meet some very unusual ladies and their very unusual menagerie, take a visit to The Island of the Aunts.

Book List:

Cherry, Lynne. *The Dragon and the Unicorn*. San Diego: Harcourt Brace, c1995, IL 3-6, RL 4.4
Valerio, the dragon, and Allegra, the unicorn, are driven into hiding when humans begin to destroy the natural beauty of their land, but hope is revived when they befriend the daughter of the man responsible.

Coville, Bruce. *The Dragonslayers*. New York: Pocket Books, c1994, IL 3-6, RL 4.6
Witch Grizelda creates a dragon so fierce it frightens even the king's knights. Who will be able to kill this creature?

Coville, Bruce. *Jeremy Thatcher, Dragon Hatcher*. San Diego: Jane Yolen Books, c1991, IL 3-6, RL 5.9
Small for his age but artistically talented, 12-year-old Jeremy Thatcher unknowingly buys a dragon's egg.

Fabrick, Harriett. *Furello*. The Woodlands, TX: Wildflower USA, c1997, IL 3-6, RL 4.8
Furello, a young unicorn, jumps out of a flower one day into an enchanted valley where he meets an old man who promises riches if Furello can find the most important thing in the world. With his new friend Kelton, the elk, Furello sets out to find it.

Gray, Luli. *Falcon's Egg*. Boston: Houghton Mifflin, c1995, IL 3-6, RL 5.9
Taking care of her younger brother and a loving, but flighty mother has made Falcon, a very responsible 11-year-old. However, she needs the help of her great-great-aunt, a friendly neighbor, and an ornithologist when she finds a unusual egg in Central Park.

Magraw, Trisha. *Princess Megan*. Portland, ME: Magic Attic Press, c1995, IL 3-6, RL 5.5
When Megan and her mother argue over plans for the weekend, she retreats to the magic attic where she becomes a princess who helps save the life of a unicorn.

Nichol, Barbara. *Dippers*. Toronto: Tundra Books, c1997, IL 3-6, RL 2.8
A young girl tells about the summer of 1912 in the city of Toronto when her sister got sick, her mother worried about losing her job, and the dippers, a furry dog-like creature with wings, came up out of the nearby Don River.

Rupp, Rebecca. *The Dragon of Lonely Island*. Cambridge, Mass.: Candlewick Press, 1998, IL 3-6, RL 7.0
Three children spend the summer with their mother on a secluded island where they discover a three-headed dragon living in a cave and learn what it means to be a Dragon Friend.

Seabrooke, Brenda. *The Care and Feeding of Dragons*. New York: Cobblehill Books, c1998, IL 3-6, RL 4.2
Follow the adventures of Alastair as he tries to protect his pet dragon, Spike, from dragonnappers while trying to adjust to his new fourth-grade teacher.

Sterman, Betsy. *Backyard Dragon*. New York: HarperCollins, c1993, IL 3-6, RL 5.7
With the help of three friends, a young boy and his grandfather help a 15th-century Welsh dragon find its way home.

Suggested Activities:

Activity #1: Paper Bag Masks

Students can create paper bag animal masks of mythical animals. A plain brown shopping bag makes a great monster mask.

You will need

- a brown paper bag (plain shopping bag)
- clear tape
- scissors
- white glue
- crayons
- an assortment of colored paper, fabric scraps, foam, feathers, tissue paper ....and almost any kind of junk that is lightweight.

1. Try on your bag, and cut slits at the four corners, so it will fit your shoulders.

2. Mark the correct position for your eyes. *Carefully*, use a pen or pencil, and poke a hole for each eye, from the inside. You can also have someone do this from the outside with a piece of tape.

3. Take off the mask and use a scissors to cut out the eye holes. You can also cut out a nose and mouth if you like.

4. Decorate your mask!

Be creative making the dragons.

Activity #2: Mythical Creatures

Mythical creatures often have some resemblance to existing animals. For instance, unicorns look similar to horses. Have the students create their own mythical creature that resembles an existing animal. They should draw the animal and explain its magical powers.

Activity #3: Dragon Myths

Have students create their own dragon or unicorn myth.

Activity #4: Creature Poems

Have students write their own poem or acrostic about dragons or unicorns.

Dragons
Rarely
Announce
Going
On
Naughty
Sojourns

Activity #5: **Dragons Around Us**

Students will be introduced to collections of folklore from around the world.

For examples of collections, see Handout #4: *Dragon Tales*.

- Students will be introduced to several variations of the same fairy tale or folktale from various parts of the world. Cinderella is a good one to choose because the students are very familiar with the story and there are numerous variations available.

- Students will discuss how these variations are similar and how they are different. They will discuss how the stories are changed to reflect the culture.

- Students will then research how dragons are portrayed in at least three different cultures.

- Students will make a drawing of each dragon.

- Students will make a list of the characteristics of the dragons in each culture (e.g. appearance, powers, origin, temperament).

- Students will research the cultural influences.

- Students will reflect on the differences in how the dragons are portrayed. They will understand the cultural influences in each portrayal.

Handout #4: Dragon Tales

Aesop's Fables. New York: H. Holt, 1999.

Hamilton, Virginia. *Her Stories: African American Folktales, Fairy Tales, And True Tales*. New York: Blue Sky Press, c1995.

Martin, Rafe. *Mysterious Tales Of Japan*. New York: G.P. Putnam's Sons, c1996.

Matthews, John. *The Barefoot Book of Giants, Ghosts and Goblins: Traditional Tales from Around the World*. New York: Barefoot Books, c1999.

Osborne, Mary Pope. *American Tall Tales*. New York: Knopf , c1991.

Shannon, George. *More True Lies: 18 Tales for You To Judge*. New York: Greenwillow Books, c2001.

Shannon, George. *True Lies: 18 Tales For You to Judge* New York: Beech Tree, 1998.

Sherman, Josepha. *Told Tales: Nine Folktales From Around The World*. New York: Silver Moon Press, c1995.

Vande Velde, Vivian. *Tales from the Brothers Grimm and the Sisters Weird*. San Diego: Harcourt Brace, c1995.

Fractured Fairy Tales

Introduction

We have all been raised on traditional fairy tales and folklores. Most of us are extremely familiar with stories such as Little Red Riding Hood or Goldilocks or Cinderella. What if we take these familiar tales and add a bit of a twist? Maybe the main character doesn't behave as we expect. Maybe there is more to the story than we thought. In this chapter, we are looking at fractured fairy tales, which are tales that have been changed in a quirky way. Remember, maybe the ugly duckling grew up to be just an ugly duck after all. Enjoy sharing these off-beat interpretations with your students and let them join the fun.

Standards Addressed (McREL)
Language Arts
Reading
Standard 6
Uses reading skills and strategies to understand and interpret a variety of literary texts

Level II Grade: 3-5

1. Uses reading skills and strategies to understand a variety of literary passages and texts (e.g., fairy tales, folktales, fiction, nonfiction, myths, poems, fables, fantasies, historical fiction, biographies, autobiographies, chapter books)

2. Knows the defining characteristics of a variety of literary forms and genres (e.g., fairy tales, folktales, fiction, nonfiction, myths, poems, fables, fantasies, historical fiction, biographies, autobiographies, chapter books)

Standards Addressed (NETS)
Performance Indicators for Technology-Literate Students

Grades 3-5

4. Use general purpose productivity tools and peripherals to support personal productivity, remediate skill deficits, and facilitate learning throughout the curriculum

5. Use technology tools (e.g., multimedia authoring, presentation, Web tools, digital cameras, scanners) for individual and collaborative writing, communication, and publishing activities to create knowledge products for audiences inside and outside the classroom

6. Use telecommunications efficiently to access remote information, communicate with others in support of direct and independent learning, and pursue personal interests

Sample Booktalk:

Scieszka, Jon. *The Stinky Cheese Man and Other Fairly Stupid Tales*. New York: Viking, 1992, IL K-3, RL 3.9

Have you ever wondered "what if"? What if things we know aren't really the way they seem? What if the familiar fairy tales we grew up with aren't they way we remember them? What if the ugly duckling grew up to be just an ugly duck? Well, Jon Scieszka has taken some very familiar fairy tales and offered his peculiar twist to them and the results are hilarious. This book may have been written for a younger crowd, but it will be enjoyed by young and old alike. Quick, let's go back and find out all about Little Red Riding Shorts, The Stinky Cheese Man and Other Fairly Stupid Tales.

Book List:

Ada, Alma Flor. *Yours Truly, Goldilocks*. New York: Atheneum Books for Young Readers, c1998, IL K-3, RL 3.5
This book presents the correspondence of Goldilocks, the three pigs, Baby Bear, Peter Rabbit, and Little Red Riding Hood as they plan to attend a housewarming party for the pigs and avoid the evil wolves in the forest.

Briggs, Raymond. *Jim and the Beanstalk*. New York: Coward McCann, 1989, IL K-3, RL 3.1
In a sequel to the original tale, Jim meets a sad and aging giant who complains some boy once climbed up the beanstalk and robbed his father. Jim tries to improve the giant's lot.

Cole, Babette. *Prince Cinders*. New York: Putnam, 1997, c1987, IL K-3, RL 2.8
A fairy grants a small, skinny prince a change in appearance and the chance to go to the Palace Disco.

Ernst, Lisa Campbell. *Little Red Riding Hood: A Newfangled Prairie Tale*. New York: Simon & Schuster Books for Young Readers, c1995, IL K-3, RL 2.9
An updated version, set on the prairie, of the familiar story about a little girl and her grandmother, this time with a not-so-clever wolf.

Lowell, Susan. *Cindy Ellen: A Wild Western Cinderella*. New York: HarperCollins, c2000, IL K-3, RL 4.0
Cindy Ellen loses one of her diamond spurs at the square dance in this wild West retelling of the classic Cinderella story.

Prater, John. *Once Upon a Time*. Cambridge, Mass.: Candlewick Press, 1995, IL K-3, RL 1.6
A bored boy's world is suddenly populated by three house-building pigs, a girl wearing a red hood, and other familiar nursery characters.

Stanley, Diane. *Rumpelstiltskin's Daughter*. New York: Morrow Junior Books, c1997, IL K-3, RL 5.5
Rumpelstiltskin's daughter may not be able to spin straw into gold, but she is more than a match for a monarch whose greed has blighted an entire kingdom.

Trivizas, Eugenios. *The Three Little Wolves and the Big Bad Pig*. New York: Margaret K. McElderry Books, c1993, IL K-3, RL 5.1
An altered version of the traditional tale about the conflict between pig and wolf—with a surprise ending.

Turkle, Brinton. *Deep in the Forest*. New York: Puffin, 1987, c1976, IL K-3
A curious bear explores a cabin in the forest, with disastrous results.

Yolen, Jane. *Sleeping Ugly*. New York: Putnam & Grosset Group, 1997, c1991, IL K-3, RL 3.1
When beautiful Princess Miserella, Plain Jane, and a fairy fall under a sleeping spell, a prince undoes the spell in a surprising way.

Activity #1: **Rewriting Fairy Tales**

Have students use traditional fairy tales and rewrite them from a different angle. They can change the main character in the story or add a different slant to the story. Changing the location or time period is a great way to rewrite a traditional fairy tale.

Activity #2: **Read All About It**

Create a newspaper in which all the stories are based on fairy tales. The students can work in groups. Each newspaper article should be written as if it were a straight news story. The students should be sure to use the 5W's of newspaper reporting. They can illustrate their "news" stories by creating drawings on the computer or by hand.

Activity #3: **Fairy Tale Presentations**

Have students retell the fairy tale using a multimedia presentation tool such as PowerPoint or Hyperstudio. They need to understand the important parts of the fairy tale (good vs. evil, moral at end, personification) and be able to illustrate it using clip art or images from the Internet.

Activity #4: **Class Fairy Tale**

Write a fairy tale as a class project. Start by writing one sentence, then pass the story from student to student, each adding one sentence. When the story is complete, read it aloud to the delight of all. Have the students share the fairy tale with other classes or post it on the class Web page.

Activity #5: **Student-Authored Fractured Fairy Tales**

Students will create their own fairy tale and then create a fractured version of it. Brainstorm the elements of a traditional fairy tale.

What elements make a fractured fairy tale?

Understand the basic elements.

Students will read some of the fractured fairy tales so they understand the concept.

Students will be familiar with a variety of fairy tales and understand the components that make up a fairy tale.

Students will use fairy tale elements such as magic, characters with magical powers, good vs. evil, and a moral to the story to create their tale.

They will also create a fractured interpretation of their tale.

They will use creative language.

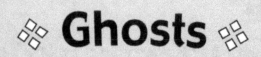

Ghosts

Introduction

Look, over there! Quick! Did you see it? No? Maybe it wasn't there. Or maybe I am the only one who can see it. Some people believe in ghosts, some don't. Whether you believe or not, everyone seems to have a fascination with ghosts. In this chapter, we look at several books about ghosts and the supernatural. Have a haunting good time as you and your students get into the spirit of these books.

Standards Addressed (McREL)
Language Arts
Reading
Standard 5
Uses the general skills and strategies of the reading process

Level II Grade: 3–5

12. Uses personal criteria to select reading material (e.g., personal interest, knowledge of authors and genres, text difficulty, recommendations of others)

Standard 6
Uses reading skills and strategies to understand and interpret a variety of literary texts

Level II Grade: 3–5

2. Knows the defining characteristics of a variety of literary forms and genres (e.g., fairy tales, folktales, fiction, nonfiction, myths, poems, fables, fantasies, historical fiction, biographies, autobiographies, chapter books)

4. Understands similarities and differences within and among literary works from various genre and cultures (e.g., in terms of settings, character types, events, point of view; role of natural phenomena)

Standards Addressed (NETS)
Performance Indicators for Technology-Literate Students

Grades 3–5

4. Use general purpose productivity tools and peripherals to support personal productivity, remediate skill deficits, and facilitate learning throughout the curriculum

5. Use technology tools (e.g., multimedia authoring, presentation, Web tools, digital cameras, scanners) for individual and collaborative writing, communication, and publishing activities to create knowledge products for audiences inside and outside the classroom

6. Use telecommunications efficiently to access remote information, communicate with others in support of direct and independent learning, and pursue personal interests

Sample Booktalk:

DeFelice, Cynthia. *Ghost Of Fossil Glen*. New York: Farrar, Strauss, Giroux, 1998. IL 3-6 , RL 6.6

Allie is sure she heard a voice. But who would be talking to her out here? She is out on a hike with no one around. She is looking for fossils and as she is going down a steep cliff, she gets stuck. She is helped off the cliff by the voice of a young girl. No one is going to believe her that the ghost of Lucy Stiles has helped her out of a bad situation. Allie learns Lucy once lived in a house near her. She finds Lucy's diary and is drawn into a mystery. This is a tale of murder and revenge. Find out what happens to Allie as she becomes involved with The Ghost of Fossil Glen.

Book List:

Cassedy, Sylvia. *Behind the Attic Wall*. New York: Crowell, c1983, IL 3-6, RL 6.0
In the bleak, forbidding house of her great-aunts, neglected 12-year-old orphan Maggie hears ghostly voices and finds magic that awakens in her the capacity to love and be loved.

Creech, Sharon. *Pleasing the Ghost*. New York: HarperCollins, c1996, IL 3-6, RL 4.8
Nine-year-old Dennis, whose uncle and father died within a year of one another, is visited by the ghost of his uncle. Together they settle some unfinished business.

Fleischman, Sid. *The Midnight Horse*. New York: Greenwillow Books, c1990, IL 3-6, RL 5.4
Touch enlists the help of the Great Chaffalo, a ghostly magician, to thwart his great-uncle's plans to put Touch into the orphan house and swindle the Red Raven Inn away from Miss Sally.

Griffith, Helen V. *Cougar*. New York: Greenwillow Books, c1999, IL 3-6, RL 3.9
Starting a new life on a farm in the country, Nickel has to adjust to the attentions of a local bully and the appearances of a ghost horse that was supposed to have died in a fire.

Murrow, Liza Ketchum. *The Ghost of Lost Island*. New York: Holiday House, c1991, IL 3-6, RL 5.5
While helping his grandfather herd and shear his flock of sheep on a small island off the coast of Maine, 12-year-old Gabe encounters a mysterious woman who may be the ghost of a drowned milkmaid.

Pearson, Kit. *Awake and Dreaming*. New York: Viking, 1996, IL 3-6, RL 6.1
Theo, the 10-year-old daughter of a young and irresponsible mother, dreams of belonging to a family with two parents and brothers and sisters. With the help of a ghostly friend, her life seems to get better.

Russell, Barbara T. *Blue Lightning*. New York: Viking, 1997, IL 3-6, RL 5.9
When a bolt of lightning provides 12-year-old Calvin with an out-of-body experience, he meets the spirit of the father he never knew. He brings a troubled ghost named Rory back to the living world with him—only to see Rory threaten his chances of pitching in a baseball game.

Shreve, Susan Richards. *Ghost Cats*. New York: A. Levine Books, 1999, IL 3-6, RL 5.2
Eleven-year-old Peter and his three younger siblings rediscover their lost closeness when the ghosts of their dead pet cats begin to mysteriously return.

Wallace, Barbara Brooks. *Ghosts in the Gallery*. New York: Atheneum Books for Young Readers, c2000, IL 3-6, RL 5.3
When 11-year-old Jenny arrives at her grandfather's house but is not recognized as one of the family because of a servant's intrigue, the young orphan endures a difficult fate.

Wright, Betty Ren. *The Moonlight Man*. New York: Scholastic Press, 2000, IL 3-6, RL 5.4
When their father moves them for the seventh time in the five years since their mother's death, Jenny and her younger sister hope to stay in this latest house and try to find out about the malevolent ghost who seems bent on getting revenge on their elderly neighbors.

Activity #1: Do You Believe in Ghosts?

Some people believe in ghosts. Some do not. Survey the class and note how many believe, how many don't and how many are unsure. Using spreadsheet software, graph the class results.

Activity #2: Ghost Story

Have the students write their own ghost story. The story should take place in the students' town or state. They can draw on stories they have heard. Be sure to include a colorful cover for the story. Before they begin, they should be instructed to think about

- The elements of a short story, including the plot development, character change, mood, setting, problem and resolution;
- The "local color" they will include that is particular to the region such as specific locations, regional plants and animals, and local idioms and dialect; and
- The use of literary devices to enhance the story (imagery, dialect, point of view, theme, word choices).

Activity #3: Ghost Mobiles

Have students work in groups to create ghost mobiles. These can be hung from the ceiling. It's fun to use glow-in-the-dark paper or stickers on the mobiles

Activity #4: Tell Me a Scary Story

Have students take turns telling ghost stories. If appropriate for the class level, turn off lights and use flashlights or glow sticks to light the room.

Activity #5: Ghost Chalk Stories

Students will read several ghost stories.
The teacher should demonstrate a chalk story.

- Students will work in small groups.
- Students will write a simple ghost story.
- Students will present the story to the class by means of a chalk story—drawing a picture on the chalkboard (or whiteboard) that gradually develops as you tell a story. It may begin as just a letter on the board or a simple stick figure. The drawing becomes more elaborate as the story goes on. At the story conclusion, the picture is complete. It does not have to be elaborate or lengthy, and the pictures can be quite simple.

Heroes

Introduction

We all need heroes. They can be as near to us as our parents and those we see every day. They can be sports figures. They can be very brave people we hear about on the news. Sometimes we look up to people as heroes who aren't really very heroic. They may be rich. They may be famous. Heroes' actions are what we should judge them on. In this chapter, we will look at different types of heroes. The students will see mythical heroes, famous heroes, and the heroes from down the street. We all must choose our heroes wisely. The activities in this section will help the students analyze what it means to be a hero.

Standards Addressed (McREL)
Language Arts
Reading
Standard 6

Uses reading skills and strategies to understand and interpret a variety of literary texts

Level II Grades 3-5:

5. Understands elements of character development in literary works (e.g., differences between main and minor characters; stereotypical characters as opposed to fully developed characters; changes that characters undergo; the importance of a character's actions, motives, and appearance to plot and theme)

Standards Addressed (NETS)
Performance Indicators for Technology-Literate Students

Grades 3-5

1. Use general purpose productivity tools and peripherals to support personal productivity, remediate skill deficits, and facilitate learning throughout the curriculum.

5. Use technology tools (e.g., multimedia authoring, presentation, Web tools, digital cameras, scanners) for individual and collaborative writing, communication, and publishing activities to create knowledge products for audiences inside and outside the classroom.

6. Use telecommunications efficiently to access remote information, communicate with others in support of direct and independent learning, and pursue personal interests.

Sample Booktalk:

Yolen, Jane. *Odysseus in the Serpent Maze*. New York: HarperCollins, c2001, IL 3-6, RL 4.7

Have you ever read a book that features an adult character and wonder what that character may have been like as a child? Jane Yolen has taken up that challenge. She has taken the character of Odysseus from Homer's epic and told us a story of what his life was like as a 13-year-old. The story opens with Odysseus visiting with his grandfather. Odysseus longs to be a hero. He and his companion, Mentor, set off on an adventure to become heroes. When their plan to kill a wild boar that has been terrorizing the village goes awry, they are left wondering what it takes to be a hero. On their way back home, they are tossed overboard and left to fend for themselves. Picked up by a pirate ship, they are introduced to Princess Helen and her handmaiden, Penelope, who have also been kidnapped by the pirates. What ensues is a satisfying tale of wondrous beasts, mythical Greek gods and, of course, heroism. Journey with these young people as we read about Odysseus in the Serpent Maze.

Book List:

Byars, Betsy Cromer. *My Dog, My Hero*. New York: H. Holt, c2000, IL 3-6, RL 5.0
A panel of three judges has to decide which dog out of eight finalists deserves to win the title of My Hero.

Fritz, Jean. *Why Not, Lafayette?* New York: G.P. Putnam's, c1999, IL 3-6, RL 5.0
This book traces the life of the French nobleman who fought for democracy in revolutions in both the United States and France.

George, Jean Craighead. *Julie of the Wolves*. New York: HarperCollins, c1972, IL 5-8, RL 5.6
While running away from home and an unwanted marriage, a 13-year-old Eskimo girl becomes lost on the North Slope of Alaska and is befriended by a wolf pack.

Jacques, Brian. *Castaways of the Flying Dutchman*. New York: Philomel, c2001, IL 5-8, RL 5.1
In 1620, a boy and his dog are rescued from the doomed ship, Flying Dutchman, by an angel who guides them in traveling the world, eternally helping those in great need.

Kelleher, D. V. *Defenders of the Universe*. Boston: Houghton Mifflin, 1993, IL 3-6, RL 4.9
A group of six children band together in a "superhero" group and eventually put their play skills to practical use.

Krensky, Stephen. *Buster Baxter, Cat Saver*. Boston: Little, Brown, c2000, IL 3-6, RL 4.3
When Buster rescues a cat stuck in a tree, he is treated like a hero. When he begins to enjoy his celebrity a little too much, his friends devise a plan to bring him back to his old self.

Mackel, Kathy. *Eggs In One Basket*. New York: HarperCollins, c2000, IL 3-6, RL 4.9
With the help of two middle-school classmates and a bear-like talking "dog" from the planet Sirius, seventh-grader Scott Schreiber discovers he can be a hero in other ways than just on the football field.

Pilkey, Dav. *The Adventures of Captain Underpants: An Epic Novel*. New York: Blue Sky Press, c1997, IL 3-6, RL 4.8
When George and Harold hypnotize their principal into thinking that he is the superhero Captain Underpants, he leads them to the lair of the nefarious Dr. Diaper, where they must defeat his evil robot henchmen.

Rodda, Emily. *Rowan of Rin*. New York: Greenwillow Books, 2001, IL 3-6, RL 3.7
Because only he can read the magical map, young, weak and timid Rowan joins six other villagers to climb a mountain and try to restore their water supply, as fears of a dragon and other horrors threaten to drive them back.

Sonenklar, Carol. *Mighty Boy*. New York: Orchard, c1999, IL 3-6, RL 5.0
When he gets a chance to meet his hero, the television character Mighty Boy, Howard Weinstein discovers his own strengths that help him handle the bully in his new fourth grade class.

Suggested Activities:

Activity #1: What is a Hero?

Have students brainstorm ideas to answer "What is a hero?" What characteristics do heroes possess? Does the person have to be famous to be a hero? Compile a list for the class to use to discuss heroes.

Activity #2: Heroes Among Us

Imagine that your local newspaper has just begun a new series to be titled "Heroes Among Us." They have asked the students to help them find deserving local heroes. Each of the students will need to nominate a candidate. They should find out something about them. What does this person do? What is her philosophy on life? Does he think of himself as a hero? Why or why not? Write a letter to the newspaper to nominate this person and include the reasons for choosing her or him.

Activity #3: My Hero

Have students tell about someone famous they think is a hero. Why do they think that person is a hero? What has the person done to be labeled a hero? Have students write a letter to the person telling why they chose that person as their hero. The letters do not really have to be sent and students should not be limited to people who are currently living.

Activity #4: Heroes in Print

Have students examine different literature books in the classroom and school library. Which ones can be said to have a hero? Compile and annotate a class list of books with annotations that can be used in the study of heroes. For examples, see: http://www.concord.k12.nh.us/schools/rundlett/heroes/herobook.html

Activity #5: Heroes Are Timeless

The students will look at heroes through the ages. There are many people who we think of as heroes who may have not been thought of as heroes during their lifetimes. Students will research heroes from the past and create simple Web pages for those heroes.

- Brainstorm the characteristics of a hero
- Students will be given the names of historical persons considered important or heroic by current standards.
- Students will be taught how to research information on the Internet.
- Students will be taught to create simple Web pages.

Students will research the life of their assigned hero. They will need to gather standard information about the person such as birth and death dates, career highlights, family. They will also need to understand why that person should be considered a hero. They will need to note URLs of Web pages that give information about the person.

Using a simple HTML composer or word processor, students will construct a Web page about their hero. Information that should be included on the Web page:

- Name of person
- Birth and death dates

- Family

- Career highlights

- Why the person is considered a hero

- Links of interest: The page should include at least three links to pages about the person.

- A picture, if available. Have the students ask permission to use the pictures or have them draw the illustrations by hand or on the computer.

Honesty

Introduction

"A man's word is his bond." Have you ever heard that expression? What it means is that it is very important to tell the truth. When you make a promise to someone, you need to keep that promise. When you tell someone something, it should be based on truth. When people lie, it often comes back to them. Being caught in a lie is a terrible thing, but not as bad as being dishonest to begin with. In this section, we will look at books that deal with the theme of honesty. The suggested activities should help reinforce the value of honesty in everyday life.

Standards Addressed (McREL)
Language Arts
Reading
Standard 6

Uses reading skills and strategies to understand and interpret a variety of literary texts

Level II Grade: 3-5

2. Knows the defining characteristics of a variety of literary forms and genres (e.g., fairy tales, folk tales, fiction, nonfiction, myths, poems, fables, fantasies, historical fiction, biographies, autobiographies, chapter books)

4. Understands similarities and differences within and among literary works from various genre and cultures (e.g., in terms of settings, character types, events, point of view; role of natural phenomena)

5. Understands elements of character development in literary works (e.g., differences between main and minor characters; stereotypical characters as opposed to fully developed characters; changes that characters undergo; the importance of a character's actions, motives, and appearance to plot and theme)

6. Makes inferences or draws conclusions about characters' qualities and actions (e.g., based on knowledge of plot, setting, characters' motives, characters' appearances, other characters' responses to a character)

9. Makes connections between characters or simple events in a literary work and people or events in his or her own life

Standard 7

Uses reading skills and strategies to understand and interpret a variety of informational texts

Level II Grade: 3-5

2. Knows the defining characteristics of a variety of informational texts (e.g., textbooks, biographical sketches, letters, diaries, directions, procedures, magazines)

Standards Addressed (NETS)

Performance Indicators for Technology-Literate Students

Grades 3–5

4. Use general purpose productivity tools and peripherals to support personal productivity, remediate skill deficits, and facilitate learning throughout the curriculum

5. Use technology tools (e.g., multimedia authoring, presentation, Web tools, digital cameras, scanners) for individual and collaborative writing, communication, and publishing activities to create knowledge products for audiences inside and outside the classroom

6. Use telecommunications efficiently to access remote information, communicate with others in support of direct and independent learning, and pursue personal interests

Sample Booktalk:

Korman, Gordon. *Liar, Liar, Pants on Fire*. New York: Scholastic, 1997. IL 3-6, RL 3.5

Zoe is finding life in third grade to be harder than she thought it would be. She doesn't think she is very interesting, so she makes up stories about herself to make her look much more interesting than she is. Everyone catches on to her lies and soon no one believes a word she says. When she finally has something interesting happen to her, no one will believe her. After all, who would believe that an eagle has made a nest in her back yard? What can she do to get rid of her reputation as a liar? Can her principal help her? Can anyone help her learn the difference between imagination and lies? Spend time with Zoe as she deals with Liar, Liar, Pants on Fire.

Book List:

Bawden, Nina. *Humbug*. New York: Clarion Books, c1992, IL 3-6, RL 6.1
When eight-year-old Cora is sent to stay next door with the seemingly pleasant woman called Aunt Sunday, she is tormented by Aunt Sunday's mean-spirited, deceitful daughter, but finds an ally in Aunt Sunday's elderly mother.

Breathed, Berke. *Edwurd Fudwupper Fibbed Big*. Boston: Little, Brown, c2000, IL 3-6, RL 4.1
Edwurd's little sister comes to the rescue when Edwurd's humongous fib lands him in trouble with a three-eyed alien from another galaxy.

Coville, Bruce. *The Skull of Truth*. San Diego: Harcourt Brace, c1997, IL 3-6, RL 6.6
Charlie, a sixth-grader with a compulsion to tell lies, acquires a mysterious skull that forces its owner to tell only the truth, causing some awkward moments before Charlie understands its power.

DeClements, Barthe. *Liar, Liar*. New York: Marshall Cavendish, c1998, IL 3-6, RL 4.2
Sixth-grader Gretchen and her friends begin to have problems when a new girl starts telling some very believable, but untrue, stories.

Fletcher, Ralph J. *Spider Boy*. New York: Bantam Doubleday Dell Books for Young Readers, 1998, c1997, IL 3-6, RL 4.8
After moving to another state, seventh-grader Bobby deals with the change by telling people at school made-up stories and then retreating into his world of pet spiders and books about spiders.

Kline, Suzy. *Mary Marony and the Chocolate Surprise*. New York: Putnam's Sons, c1995, IL 3-6, RL 4.9
Mary decides it's all right to cheat to make sure she wins a special lunch with her favorite teacher, but the results of her dishonesty end up surprising the whole second-grade class.

Martin, Ann M. *Jessi and the Awful Secret.* New York: Scholastic, c1993, IL 3-6, RL 5.2
Jessi volunteers to help out in a ballet class for children. While helping, Jessi discovers a secret about Mary, one that could hurt her. Jessi has to decide if she should tell anyone and risk losing a friendship.

Pfeffer, Susan Beth. *The Pizza Puzzle.* New York: Bantam Doubleday Dell Books for Young Readers, 1997, c1996, IL 3-6, RL 4.8
Distracted by her worries that her parents may get a divorce, Taryn gets in trouble with her seventh-grade English teacher and is caught up in an increasingly complicated series of lies.

Shreve, Susan Richards. *Jonah, the Whale.* New York: Arthur A. Levine Books, c1998., IL 3-6, RL 5.8
After moving to a new town, Jonah, an 11-year-old with a big imagination, reinvents himself as a talk show host, hoping this will somehow bring his absent father back.

Spinner, Stephanie. *Be First in the Universe.* New York: Delacorte Press, c2000, IL 3-6, RL 5.9
While staying with their hippie grandparents, 10-year-old twins Tod and Tessa discover an unusual shop at the nearby mall, where they find a lie-detecting electronic pet, a Do-Right machine, and other alien gadgets that help them foil their nemeses, the evil Gneiss twins.

Suggested Activities:

Activity #1: **Hard To Be Honest**

Have students write in their journals about a time they were faced with a hard decision about being honest. Have them write about a time they told the truth even though it was a difficult thing to do.

Activity #3: **I Did It**

Have students write in their journals about a time they took responsibility for something they had done or said.

Activity #3: **What Would You Do?**

Have the students discuss or write about different scenarios that involve honesty. For example:

- You find a necklace on the playground. What are your options?
- You forgot your lunch ticket, and your friend drops his on the floor. You know that he has money to buy lunch. Should you use it?
- You can see the test paper of the student next to you, and you cannot think of the answer to number three. Do you copy?

See Handout #5: *Honesty Decision*

Activity #4: **I Read It in the Paper, Honest!**

Students should scan newspapers to find clippings that involve honesty. They should clip them and bring them in. The clippings can be posted around the room or put together to make a book for the class.

Activity #5: **Honestly, I Found It**

We are all basically honest people. Some of us are just a little better at remembering than others! One of the best ways to ensure that we behave in an honest way in any situation is to practice. If we know right from wrong, we are better able to make the correct decision. Talk about what it means to be honest. Brainstorm situations where it is easy to be honest and others when it is hard to be honest. Give students simple scenarios to discuss. What is the honest thing to do in each case?

Students will come up with a scenario of their own to demonstrate a situation in which honesty is involved. They will create a script for the situation. They will act out the skit for the class but stop before the final resolution of the problem. A class discussion will follow dealing with the scenario and the best resolution of the situation.

Handout #5: Honesty Decision

Scenario	Options	Action

Humorous Stories

Introduction

Everyone needs a good laugh now and again. It is said laughter is the best medicine. If this is true, here is a collection of novels that will be sure to cure even the worst mood. Students will enjoy reading about the funny things kids do. They can then continue the laughs through the classroom activities.

Standards Addressed (McREL)
Language Arts
Reading
Standard 6
Uses reading skills and strategies to understand and interpret a variety of literary texts

Level II Grade: 3–5

5. Understands elements of character development in literary works (e.g., differences between main and minor characters; stereotypical characters as opposed to fully developed characters; changes that characters undergo; the importance of a character's actions, motives, and appearance to plot and theme)

8. Understands the ways in which language is used in literary texts (e.g., personification, alliteration, onomatopoeia, simile, metaphor, imagery, hyperbole, beat, rhythm)

9. Makes connections between characters or simple events in a literary work and people or events in his or her own life

Standards Addressed (NETS)
Performance Indicators for Technology-Literate Students

Grades 3–5

4. Use general purpose productivity tools and peripherals to support personal productivity, remediate skill deficits, and facilitate learning throughout the curriculum

5. Use technology tools (e.g., multimedia authoring, presentation, Web tools, digital cameras, scanners) for individual and collaborative writing, communication, and publishing activities to create knowledge products for audiences inside and outside the classroom

6. Use telecommunications efficiently to access remote information, communicate with others in support of direct and independent learning, and pursue personal interests

Sample Booktalk:

Horvath, Polly. *When the Circus Came to Town*. New York: Farrar Strauss & Giroux, 1996. IL 3-6, RL 5.9

Ten-year-old Ivy lives in a small, quiet town where not much happens. Every day is pretty much like every other day. That is, until the Halibuts move in next door. You see, the Halibuts are circus people, which are certainly not the kind of people the townsfolk will welcome with open arms. Next, Elmira the Snake Lady moves into town. After that, the whole family of Flying Gambinis moves in. What is happening to this town? In this humorous book, Ivy tells us how life changed in Springfield. Find out what happens When the Circus Came to Town.

Book List:

Blume, Judy. *Superfudge*. New York: Bantam Doubleday Dell Books for Young Readers, 1991, c1980, IL 3-6, RL 4.2
Peter describes the highs and lows of life with his younger brother, Fudge.

Bunting, Eve. *Nasty Stinky Sneakers*. New York: HarperCollins, c1994, IL 3-6, RL 3.9
Will ten-year-old Colin find his missing stinky sneakers in time to enter the Stinkiest Sneakers in the World contest?

Conford, Ellen. *Annabel the Actress Starring in Gorilla My Dreams*. New York: Simon & Schuster Books for Young Readers, c1999, IL 3-6, RL 5.7
Though a little disappointed her first acting part is to be a gorilla at a birthday party, Annabel is determined to really get into the role.

Fitzgerald, John Dennis. *The Great Brain*. New York: Dial Books for Young Readers, c2000, IL 3-6, RL 4.8
The exploits of the Great Brain of Adenville, Utah, are described by his younger brother, frequently the victim of the Great Brain's schemes for gaining prestige or money.

Gauthier, Gail. *A Year with Butch and Spike*. New York: Putnam, c1998, IL 3-6, RL 7.8
Upon entering the sixth grade, straight-A student Jasper falls under the spell of the dreaded, irrepressible Cootch cousins.

Kline, Suzy. *Herbie Jones and the Class Gift*. New York: Puffin Books, 1989, c1987, IL 3-6, RL 4.4
Disaster strikes when Annabelle entrusts Herbie Jones and Raymond with the job of picking up the class's gift to their teacher.

Korman, Gordon. *The 6th Grade Nickname Game*. New York: Hyperion Paperbacks for Children, 2000, c1998, IL 3-6, RL 4.8
Eleven-year-old best friends Jeff and Wiley, who like to give nicknames to their classmates, try to find the right one for the new girl, Cassandra, while adjusting to the football coach who has become their new teacher.

Lowry, Lois. *See You Around, Sam!* New York: Bantam Doubleday Dell Books for Young Readers, 1998, c1996, IL 3-6, RL 4.2
Sam Krupnik, mad at his mother because she won't let him wear his new plastic fangs in the house, decides to run away to Alaska.

Park, Barbara. *Skinnybones*. New York: Random House, c1997, IL 3-6, RL 4.1
Alex's active sense of humor helps him get along with the school braggart, make the most of his athletic talents, and simply get by in a hectic world.

Pullman, Philip. *I Was a Rat!* New York: Knopf, Distributed by Random House, 2000, c1999, IL 3-6, RL 5.4
A little boy turns life in London upside down when he appears at the house of a lonely old couple and insists he was a rat.

Suggested Activities:

Activity #1: Joke Book

Create a class joke book. Students will each come up with their favorite joke, riddle or funny story. These should be word processed and illustrated if appropriate. The pages will be bound together into a class joke book that will be added to the class library.

Activity #2: Book Jacket

Have students design a book jacket that highlights a particularly important scene and reflects the mood of the book.

Activity #3: Booktalk

Have students prepare a booktalk about their book. The booktalk should include information about the author and title and also enough of the story so others will want to read it. The booktalk should end on a cliffhanger that will make the audience want more. Small passages from the book can be read to the class but should be kept to a minimum.

Activity #4: Graffiti

Create a "brick" wall on one wall of the classroom using butcher paper. Students can write graffiti that reflects a character in the book they read.

Activity #5: Kids Book Beat

Students may like to discuss their book with others. In this lesson, they will have a chance to be a "professional" book reviewer on a "television" show.

- Students will read a book.
- The classroom will be set up for the taping of the show. Two or three chairs can be placed in the front of the room for the reviewers. The other chairs can be arranged for the audience.
- Students will take turns being the on-camera talent. They will review their book and perhaps discuss it with the other on-camera talent. Audience participation is encouraged but kept low-key and dignified, not rowdy as in many of the talk shows.
- The show can be videotaped for future viewing.
- The on-camera talent and videotaper should rotate until everyone has had a turn.

Mystery and Horror

Introduction

It was a dark and stormy night, when suddenly the stillness was shattered by the sound of a blood-curdling scream. What has happened? Can you figure it out? There is nothing like a good mystery. You look at the clues and put it all together just like a puzzle. And, of course, you are always right, aren't you? In this chapter, we will look at some good mysteries. Have the students try to figure out the mystery before the end of the book. Do you have some good detectives in your class? See if you can solve some of these mysteries.

Standards Addressed (McREL)
Language Arts
Reading
Standard 5

Uses the general skills and strategies of the reading process

Level II Grade: 3-5

12. Uses personal criteria to select reading material (e.g., personal interest, knowledge of authors and genres, text difficulty, recommendations of others)

Standard 6

Uses reading skills and strategies to understand and interpret a variety of literary texts

Level II Grade: 3-5

2. Knows the defining characteristics of a variety of literary forms and genres (e.g., fairy tales, folk tales, fiction, nonfiction, myths, poems, fables, fantasies, historical fiction, biographies, autobiographies, chapter books)

4. Understands similarities and differences within and among literary works from various genre and cultures (e.g., in terms of settings, character types, events, point of view; role of natural phenomena)

Standards Addressed (NETS)
Performance Indicators for Technology-Literate Students

Grades 3-5

4. Use general purpose productivity tools and peripherals to support personal productivity, remediate skill deficits, and facilitate learning throughout the curriculum

5. Use technology tools (e.g., multimedia authoring, presentation, Web tools, digital cameras, scanners) for individual and collaborative writing, communication, and publishing activities to create knowledge products for audiences inside and outside the classroom

6. Use telecommunications efficiently to access remote information, communicate with others in support of direct and independent learning, and pursue personal interests

Sample Booktalk:

Hale, Bruce. *The Mystery of Mr. Nice: A Chet Gecko Mystery*. San Diego: Harcourt, Inc, 2000. IL 3-6, RL 4.5

Chet Gecko's my name. Solving crime is my game. I'm actually a misunderstood artist. After all, who but me could have put the "art" in smart aleck? But that's another story. Today I have something else on my mind. You see, our principal, Mr. Zero, is actually being nice to me. Now, faster than a group of kids chasing an ice cream truck, I figure out that something is funny here. No way is this cat ever nice to anyone, especially me! There has got to be a switch-a-roo going down here. This cat has got to be an imposter. And who are these new teachers here at our school? Now I'll be busier than a bunny at an all-you-can-eat salad bar trying to find out what's going on. And why is the PTA meeting so important? Join my trusty sidekick, Natalie Attired, and me as we try to solve The Mystery of Mr. Nice.

Book List:

Bailey, Linda. *How Can I Be a Detective If I Have to Baby-Sit?* Morton Grove, Ill.: A. Whitman, 1996, c1993, IL 3-6, RL 5.2
While staying with her father at a tree-planting camp in the Canadian wilderness, 12-year-old Stevie discovers she can combine babysitting with detective work.

Bunting, Eve. *Coffin on a Case*. New York: HarperCollins, c1992, IL 3-6, RL 5.2
Twelve-year-old Henry Coffin, the son of a private investigator, helps a beautiful high school girl in her dangerous attempt to find her kidnapped mother.

DeFelice, Cynthia C. *The Light on Hogback Hill*. New York: Macmillan, c1993, IL 3-6, RL 5.4
When she investigates the mysterious light up on Hogback Hill, 11-year-old Hadley finds and befriends a hunchbacked old woman with a tragic past.

Fleischman, Sid. *Jim Ugly*. New York: Greenwillow Books, c1992, IL 3-6, RL 5.8
This book chronicles the adventures of 12-year-old Jake and Jim Ugly, his father's part-mongrel, part-wolf dog, as they travel through the Old West trying to find out what really happened to Jake's actor father.

Giff, Patricia Reilly. *Kidnap at the Catfish Café*. New York: Viking, 1998, RL 3.5
Assisted by her cat Max, sixth-grader Minnie starts up her new detective agency by investigating a kidnapping and a thief who will steal anything, even a hot stove.

Howe, James. *Dew Drop Dead: A Sebastian Barth Mystery*. New York: Atheneum, c1990, IL 3-6, RL 5.5
While setting up a homeless shelter at the church, Sebastian and his friends Corrie and David solve the mystery of a dead man found in an abandoned inn.

Kline, Suzy. *Orp and the FBI*. New York: G.P. Putnam's Sons, c1995, IL 3-6, RL 4.0
Twelve-year-old Orville and his friend Derrick form their own detective agency and, with help from Orville's younger sister Chloe, investigate the arrival of an unusual letter and the appearance of a mysterious intruder.

Pevsner, Stella. *Would My Fortune Cookie Lie?* New York: Clarion Books, c1996, IL 3-6, RL 4.8
While worrying her mom is plotting to move the family from their Chicago home, 13-year-old Alexis also wonders about the mysterious young man who seems to be shadowing her friend and her.

Roberts, Willo Davis. *The Kidnappers: A Mystery*. New York: Atheneum Books for Young Readers, c1998, IL 3-6, RL 5.9
No one believes 11-year-old Joey, who has a reputation for telling tall tales, when he claims to have witnessed the kidnapping of the class bully outside their expensive New York City private school.

Walker, Paul Robert. *The Sluggers Club: A Sports Mystery.* San Diego: Harcourt Brace Jovanovich, c1993, IL 3-6, RL 5.1
When baseball equipment starts disappearing from B.J.'s Little League team, he and his friends form the Sluggers Club to investigate the crime.

Suggested Activities:

Activity #1: **Mystery Theater**

Don't you just love a good mystery? In this activity, students will create a mystery and act it out. The mystery will be videotaped so the tape can be paused when being viewed. The audience will attempt to solve the mystery before the ending is revealed.

- Students will brainstorm the necessary elements of a mystery (e.g. clues should not be mis-leading, no unfair surprises).
- Students will review how to write dialog.
- Students will learn to use a video camera.
- Students will be divided up into groups.
- Students will write a mystery story.
- Students will create a script from their story.
- Students will assign roles and act out their story.
- Students will videotape their presentation.
- When sharing the video with the class, students should stop the video before the mystery is solved. The class should try to guess the mystery's solution.

Activity #2: **Mystery Stories**

Create a real-life mystery for your class. Remember you will need to provide enough clues to enable the students to solve the mystery. Brainstorm the steps needed to solve the mystery. Students can work in groups to solve the mystery.

Activity #3: **Secret Code**

Many times, mysteries involve code writing. Have students work in groups to create a coded message. The students need to create their own code language with an answer key as well as a coded message. These can be exchanged between groups for others to try decode.

Activity #4: **Dictionary of Mysterious Words**

While reading mystery books, students should make note of the vocabulary words that seem to relate to the genre. The students can look up the definitions of these words. Compile the list into an official class Dictionary of Mysterious Words. See Handout #5: *Mystery Words.*

Handout #6: Mystery Words

Mystery Word	Definition

Activity #5: Detective Agency

Have students work in groups to create their own detective agency. They should come up with a name, a logo, the motto, and a list of the qualifications of the detectives and their areas of specialization. Create a newspaper or radio advertisement to entice clients to use your agency. See Handout #7: *Detective Agency.*

Planning Guide For Detective Agency

Name of Agency: Be sure the name reflects your personality and what you hope to specialize in. For example, Missing Pet Agency would be a good name for an agency who is looking for missing pets. Be creative.

Motto: Most companies create a motto to identify the agency. Statements such as "We love to see you smile" and "Leave no child behind" show what the company hopes to achieve. Create a snappy motto that states what you will do.

Qualifications: What makes you qualified to do the work you are advertising? Do you have the education, the experience or other things that make us want to hire you? You can list cases that you have solved in the past and prior experiences to show you are qualified.

Area of Specialization: Let us know when we should use your services. Do you just look for missing pets? Do you search for lost notebooks or other objects? Do you hunt down criminals? Be sure to add these services to your advertisement.

Sketch out your ad here or write your radio script. You will want to use a new sheet for your final copy.

Introduction

School is something we all are familiar with. Some have good feelings about school and some have feelings that are not so positive. These books and activities are meant to showcase school in a positive light and allow students to have a good feeling about their school.

Standards Addressed (McREL)
Language Arts
Reading
Standard 6
Uses reading skills and strategies to understand and interpret a variety of literary texts

Level II Grade: 3-5

5. Understands elements of character development in literary works (e.g., differences between main and minor characters; stereotypical characters as opposed to fully developed characters; changes that characters undergo; the importance of a character's actions, motives, and appearance to plot and theme)

7. Knows themes that recur across literary works

Standards Addressed (NETS)
Performance Indicators for Technology-Literate Students

Grades 3-5

4. Use general purpose productivity tools and peripherals to support personal productivity, remediate skill deficits, and facilitate learning throughout the curriculum

5. Use technology tools (e.g., multimedia authoring, presentation, Web tools, digital cameras, scanners) for individual and collaborative writing, communication, and publishing activities to create knowledge products for audiences inside and outside the classroom

6. Use telecommunications efficiently to access remote information, communicate with others in support of direct and independent learning, and pursue personal interests

Sample Booktalk:

Hill, Kirkpatrick. *The Year of Miss Agnes*. New York: M.K. McElderry Books, 2000. IL 3-6, RL 4.2

Do you have a favorite teacher? One who taught you more than just how to spell? Someone who taught you a bit about life? About yourself? Well, Miss Agnes is that kind of teacher. The year is 1948. World War II has ended and the people of the country are trying to put it behind them. But for those in the village of Koyukuk, Alaska, the war is remote. Their life is always hard and their traditions strong. It is difficult to keep a teacher in this village. The last one left claiming she couldn't stand the smell of fish that lingered around the students. The students are sure they won't need to have a new teacher.

Haven't they already been through all the available ones? Who else would be willing to come to such a small village to teach a handful of kids? Then Miss Agnes shows up. She isn't like the other teachers. She doesn't mind the smell of fish. She enjoys the local traditions. She values her students. She is different, but different in a positive way. The first thing she does is to throw away the textbooks. She has her own ideas about how to teach. The children don't quite know what to make of her, but they know she is planning to stay only one year. She has decided to return to her home in England. Will the children find a new appreciation for their school? Will Miss Agnes be able to help them learn? Find out as we spend The Year of Miss Agnes.

Book List:

Blume, Judy. *Freckle Juice*. New York: Simon & Schuster Books for Young Readers, c1971, IL 3-6, RL 3.6
Andrew wants freckles so badly that he buys Sharon's freckle recipe for 50 cents.

Clements, Andrew. *The Landry News: A Brand New School Story*. New York: Simon & Schuster Books for Young Readers, c1999, IL 3-6, RL 6.1
A fifth-grader starts a newspaper with an editorial that makes her tired classroom teacher excited about teaching again. As a result, the teacher is later threatened with disciplinary action.

Fine, Anne. *Flour Babies*. New York: Bantam Doubleday Dell Books for Young Readers, 1995, c1992, IL 5-8, RL 6.2
When his class of underachievers is assigned to spend three weeks of torture taking care of their own "babies" in the form of bags of flour, Simon makes amazing discoveries about himself while coming to terms with his long-absent father.

Fletcher, Ralph J. *Flying Solo*. New York: Clarion Books, c1998, IL 5-8, RL 5.8
Rachel, having chosen to be mute following the sudden death of a classmate, shares responsibility for their actions with the other sixth-graders who decide not to report that the substitute teacher failed to show up.

Gantos, Jack. *Heads or Tails: Stories from the Sixth Grade*. New York: Farrar Straus Giroux, 1994, IL 5-8, RL 4.9
Jack's diary helps him deal with his problems which include dog-eating alligators, a terror for an older sister, a younger brother who keeps breaking parts of himself, and next-door neighbors who are really weird.

Gantos, Jack. *Joey Pigza Swallowed the Key*. New York: Farrar, Straus and Giroux, 1998, IL 5-8, RL 5.2
To the constant disappointment of his mother and his teachers, Joey has trouble paying attention or controlling his mood swings when his prescription medications wear off and he starts getting worked up.

Klise, Kate. *Regarding the Fountain: A Tale, in Letters, of Liars and Leaks*. New York: Avon Books, c1998, IL 5-8, RL 4.8
When the principal asks a fifth-grader to write a letter regarding the purchase of a new drinking fountain for their school, chaos results.

Konigsburg, E. L. *The View from Saturday.* New York: Atheneum Books for Young Readers, c1996, IL 3-6, RL 4.8
Four students, with their own individual stories, develop a special bond and attract the attention of their teacher, a paraplegic, who chooses them to represent their sixth-grade class in the Academic Bowl competition.

Mills, Claudia. *Standing up to Mr. O.* New York: Farrar Straus Giroux, 1998, IL 3-6, RL 6.3
Twelve-year-old Maggie comes to dread biology class because her favorite teacher is insisting that she dissect a worm, an assignment that makes her feel squeamish and awakens her to the question of animal rights.

Robinson, Barbara. *The Best School Year Ever.* New York: HarperCollins, c1994, IL 3-6, RL 5.4
The six horrible Herdmans, the worst students in the history of the world, cause mayhem throughout the school year.

Suggested Activities:

Activity #1: **Classroom Rules**

Have students talk about classroom rules. Brainstorm some rules that might be applicable in the classroom. Come up with a list of rules for the class. Students should copy the rules in their notebooks and they should be posted in the classroom. Have the students keep the rules positive in nature.

For example:

Be respectful of yourself and others.

Raise your hand before you speak during a classroom lesson.

Listen quietly while others are speaking.

Activity #2: **Class News**

Have students write articles for a class newspaper to be sent home to parents. Students should write about things that are happening in the class as well as in the school. Perhaps turn the newspaper into a Web page if applicable.

Activity #3: **Different Ending**

Have students write an alternative ending to the book they have read dealing with school.

Activity #4: **Story Chains**

Students should be able to retell a story, recreate the correct sequence of events, and highlight important events. Story chains will be used to demonstrate this.

■ Students will read one of the novels as a class.

■ Prepare numerous 1" by 8 1/2" pastel-colored paper strips.

- Have students work in groups of four and assign each group a section of the novel or the entire book. Each student should get five strips. There should be one extra strip per group.

- On the extra strip, one of the students should write the title and author of the book.

- On each of the remaining strips, each student should write a sentence or two detailing important events or main ideas from the reading selection or novel. Remind them to include events from the beginning, the middle, and the end of the selection. The chosen events should summarize the novel.

- When all the strips are completed, the students are to staple or glue them in an interlocking chain, similar to holiday paper chains.

- Have students share their chains with the class.

- Use the chains to decorate a bulletin board or hang them in the hallway for all the students in your building to enjoy.

Activity #5: Comic Strip

Students will write about a funny thing that happened in school. They will then expand this into a cartoon or comic strip. The dialog should be put into dialog balloons. See Handout #8: *My Comic Strip*

My Comic Strip

Sports

Introduction

Take me out to the ball game. Play ball! Gooooooaaaaaalllll! There is nothing like a sports game to bring out the kid in everyone. Students will love reading about children their age playing the sports they love. Students need to realize, however, that not everyone is a born athlete. Not everyone can make the team, but students should be encouraged to try. In this chapter, we will be looking at sports stories — some humorous and some serious. The students will participate in classroom activities dealing with sports and the people who play them.

Standards Addressed (McREL)
Language Arts
Reading
Standard 6
Uses reading skills and strategies to understand and interpret a variety of literary texts

Level II Grade: 3–5

5. Understands elements of character development in literary works (e.g., differences between main and minor characters; stereotypical characters as opposed to fully developed characters; changes that characters undergo; the importance of a character's actions, motives, and appearance to plot and theme)

7. Knows themes that recur across literary works

Standards Addressed (NETS)
Performance Indicators for Technology-Literate Students

Grades 3–5

4. Use general purpose productivity tools and peripherals to support personal productivity, remediate skill deficits, and facilitate learning throughout the curriculum

5. Use technology tools (e.g., multimedia authoring, presentation, Web tools, digital cameras, scanners) for individual and collaborative writing, communication, and publishing activities to create knowledge products for audiences inside and outside the classroom

6. Use telecommunications efficiently to access remote information, communicate with others in support of direct and independent learning, and pursue personal interests

Sample Booktalk:

Napoli, Donna Jo. *Soccer Shock.* New York: Puffin Books, 1991. IL 3-6, RL 5.9

Adam has only one goal in mind — to make the soccer team. It is all he thinks about. But does he even stand a chance of making the team? It's becoming more and more doubtful. The coach yells at him all the time to pay more attention. Adam just knows he won't make the team. When he is walking home from practice, he is almost struck by lightning. Fortunately, he survives the experience, but soon he begins to hear strange voices. Can it be? Are the voices really coming from where he thinks? Yes, his freckles are talking to him! Read Soccer Shock to find out what the freckles have to say.

Book List:

Alexander, Nina. *Alison Rides the Rapids.* Portland, OR: Magic Attic Press, c1998, IL 3-6, RL 5.7
When a disastrous math test shakes her self-confidence, Alison goes through the magic mirror and finds her skills and courage tested as a junior river guide on a white-water rafting trip.

Avi. *S.O.R. Losers.* New York: Atheneum Books for Young Readers, c1984, IL 5-8, RL 5.0
Each member of the South Orange River seventh-grade soccer team has qualities of excellence, but not on the soccer field.

Christopher, Matt. *Wheel Wizards.* Boston: Little, Brown, c2000, IL 3-6, RL 5.2
Angry and unhappy because he is now in a wheelchair and apparently no longer able to play basketball, 12-year-old Seth is amazed to discover wheelchair basketball and finds his life is not over after all.

Gutman, Dan. *Babe and Me: A Baseball Card Adventure.* New York: Avon Books, c2000, IL 5-8, RL 5.2
With their ability to travel through time using vintage baseball cards, Joe and his father have the opportunity to find out whether Babe Ruth really did call his shot when he hit that home run in the third game of the 1932 World Series against the Chicago Cubs.

Hughes, Dean. *Home Run Hero.* New York: Atheneum Books for Young Readers, c1999, IL 3-6, RL 5.5
The players on his summer league baseball team, the Scrappers, have some talent, but Wilson is discouraged because they have an attitude problem and trouble working together as a team.

Petersen, P. J. *White Water.* New York: Simon & Schuster Books for Young Readers, c1997, IL 5-8, RL 4.8
Greg confronts his own fears and assumes a leadership role when his father is bitten by a rattlesnake during a white-water rafting trip.

Rowling, J. K. *Quidditch Through the Ages.* New York: Arthur A. Levine Books, 2001, IL 5-8, RL 6.9
A copy of a book from the library at Hogwart's, the school where Harry Potter and other young wizards receive their training, provides information about the history and conduct of Quidditch, a sport played by competing teams on flying brooms. Proceeds from this book will go to Comic Relief U.K.

Walker, Paul Robert. *The Sluggers Club: A Sports Mystery.* San Diego: Harcourt Brace Jovanovich, c1993, IL 3-6, RL 5.1
When baseball equipment starts disappearing from B.J.'s Little League team, he and his friends form the Sluggers Club to investigate the crime.

Weaver, Will. *Striking Out*. New York: HarperTrophy, 1993, IL 5-8, RL 5.1
Since the death of his older brother, 13-year-old Billy Baggs has had a distant relationship with his father. Life on their farm in northern Minnesota begins to change when he starts to play baseball.

Girls Got Game: Sports Stories & Poems. New York: H. Holt, 2001, IL 5-8, RL 6.5
A collection of short stories and poems written by and about young women in sports.

Suggested Activities:

Activity #1: Game of Your Own

Working in groups, have students come up with their own sports game. They need to include a basic set of rules and equipment needed.

Activity #2: Athlete Interview

Have students make up an interview with a famous athlete. What questions would you ask? What might the answers be?

Activity #3: Be a Winner

What does it mean to be a winner? Have students write about a time they felt like a winner.

Activity #4: Sports Trivia

Working in groups, have students create a sports trivia game. Using index cards, students should write a sports trivia question on one side and the answer on the other. These trivia questions can be taken from standard reference sources in the library media center. Students should put the citation on the answer side of the card. Students should exchange questions and try to answer them.

Activity #5: Ace Sports Reporter

You have been hired as a sports reporter for the local newspaper. Your first assignment is to cover a game for a sport you have never even heard of. You will write the newspaper coverage of the game and try to explain it as you go along. In this activity, students will have an opportunity to create their own sport. They will not have to come up with complete rules and descriptions. They will be asked to write a newspaper account of one game.

- Students will be instructed to invent a new game. It can be a variation of an existing game but should include some unusual elements.

- Students will write a newspaper article describing the game. They should include information about the players, the teams, descriptions of some of the action, and other details that will help the reader understand the game

❖ Index ❖

Printed in the USA
CPSIA information can be obtained
at www.ICGtesting.com
LVHW080723170724
785510LV00007B/289

9 781586 831066